A·G·A·I·N·S·T
G·R·A·V·I·T·Y

BY DONALD EVERETT AXINN

Sliding down the Wind (1978)
The Hawk's Dream and Other Poems (1982)
A·G·A·I·N·S·T
  G·R·A·V·I·T·Y (1986)

A★G★A★I★N★S★T G★R★A★V★I★T★Y

Poems 1982–1985

DONALD EVERETT AXINN

GROVE PRESS, INC./NEW YORK

Copyright © 1986 by Donald Everett Axinn

All rights reserved.

No part of this book may be reproduced, stored in a retrieval system, or transmitted in any form, by any means, including mechanical, electronic, photocopying, recording or otherwise, without prior written permission of the publisher.

First Grove Press Edition 1986
First Printing 1986
ISBN: 0-394-55342-X
Library of Congress Catalog Card Number 86-271

First Evergreen Edition 1986
First Printing 1986
ISBN: 0-394-62198-0
Library of Congress Catalog Card Number 86-271

Library of Congress Cataloging in Publication Data

Axinn, Donald Everett
    Against gravity.

    I. Title.
PS3551.X5A7   1986   811'.54   86-271
ISBN 0-394-55342-X
ISBN 0-394-62198-0 (Evergreen : pbk.)

Printed in the United States of America

Grove Press, Inc., 196 West Houston Street, New York, N.Y. 10014

5 4 3 2 1

*This book is dedicated to
the maker of gravity.*

*And to poets who explore and
search, to understand.*

*Also for my father, Michael,
who first took me into
the wind and above the clouds.*

ACKNOWLEDGMENTS

My appreciation to the editors of the following publications in which these poems first appeared:

Writers Forum: "Daughter's Farewell"
"Desert, Tucson to Phoenix"
"Old Pilots in Springtime"

Confrontation: "Chorus"
"Stalls"

Middlebury Magazine: "Return to the Long Trail"

Phi Beta Kappa Key Notes: "Turn-On"

The Poetry Miscellany: "In the Fall, Fire in the Trees"

Sunstorm: "Pilot"

Super Cub Pilots Newsletter: "Old Pilots in Springtime"

Xanadu: "In Clam Heaven"
"The Meadow"

My deepest thanks to Bill Matthews for his excellence as editor, and my other friends whose encouragement is so meaningful. Again to Grove Press, Bread Loaf Writers Conference, Poets and Writers, and Dianne Francis.

And especially to Joan whose support is more than that of mate and friend.

CONTENTS

Author's Preface   xi
Pilot   3
In the Fall, Fire in the Trees   6
Cumuli   8
Pond Bay, B.V.I.   10
Turn-on   12
Reflection   14
In this House   16
Orange Crate on a Dawn Patrol vs. the Red Baron   18
Miami Beach Art Show   23
Forgetting Jesse Carpenter   26
The Suck of the Glades   28
voice of memory   32
In My Father's Closet   33
White   34
Antique Story   36
Desert, Tucson to Phoenix   38
Storm   40
Storm Sequence   42
Clouds   43
The Fog   44
The Well of Jacob   45
Late Monday Afternoon, Just Before the Rain   46
The Meadow   48
Genesis   50
Sunset on the Amtrak, Lorton to Sanford   52
Old Pilots in Springtime   54
Mallard's Wife   55
Tree   56
Chorus   58
Forgetting   59
Return to the Long Trail   60

In Clam Heaven   62
Stalls   64
Search   66
Daughter's Farewell   68
Time to Fly   69
Impossible Tasks   71

Author's Preface

The baby squeals, gently tossed and suspended for minute seconds, confident that strong hands will catch her and prevent the crash to earth. The diver arches into the air, free, his twists and tumbles graceful until he returns to the water and earth, once again joining the rest of us. The scuba diver glides through water, his weightlessness the balance he seeks and achieves. And consider the pilot who sails through the air, plane or glider his medium, freed for a limited time from earth's constraints and all he has left below. Or the astronaut who floats with perfect ease, unbound by the gravity that controls every material thing.

Gravity controls our lives from the moment we drop from the suspension in our mother's womb to our final fall when we are plunged by gravity under the surface of the earth on which we have lived in some kind of inexact balance. We learn early on to contend with gravity, but understanding it is something else, for gravity can be identified more easily than it can be explained. Isaac Newton said, "Gravity must be caused by an agent acting constantly according to certain laws, but whether this agent be material or immaterial is a question I have left to the consideration of my readers."[1] Perhaps the best way to deal with this phenomenon is through art, there to wrestle with the intangible and unknown through intuition and instinct, experience and experiment. To explore the unknown and organize some meaning out of the confusion often seems arrogant, the process awesome, frustrating, even humorous. There are those times, however, if we become free we can move against gravity, against the force that is neither good nor evil.

Newton, "carpenter of the invisible"[2], established essential laws of gravity, introducing its definitions to an ignorant world. But Newton was as perplexed in trying to clarify and interpret gravity as we are today. "You sometimes speak of gravity as essential and inherent to matter. Pray do not ascribe that notion to me, for the cause of gravity is what I do not pretend to know."[3] His conclusion about the cosmos was that there is no vacuum or void: "I suppose that there is diffused through all places an aethereal substance capable of contraction and dilation, strongly elastic, and in a word much like air in all respects, but far more subtle."[4] More subtle, yes, much more. And complicated by the amplification of Albert Einstein, whose theory of relativity characterizes gravity as a manifestation of curved spacetime.

Gravity is indeed a strange kind of kinetic energy which cannot be seen or touched. Being free from it, whether it is physical or emotional, fantasized or actual, occurs when we push against gravity, which is measured by the extent of our counterforce and motivation. Sometimes there is a state of ecstasy, be it short or long, and we enter a dream-like existence. Often it is only in dreams we are free to be and do perhaps what we unconsciously wish, to be unbound from another kind of gravity.

If it happens, we come to "know" the merging of some universal essence into a very specific thing or image. The result is a kind of aesthetic moment, the more seamless, the more perfect. When we find ourselves confused or troubled, art in a form like poetry seems required because it provides us with truths we need to frame our lives around, often with hope, often with escape from the pains of existence. In that way, we make mirrors in which it is possible to catch glimpses of ourselves.

Donald Everett Axinn
Long Island, New York

[1] *Correspondence* ..., III, p. 254.
[2] An expression by Nancy Willard.
[3] *Correspondence* ..., III, p. 240.
[4] Attributed to conversation with Robert Boyle.

A★G★A★I★N★S★T
G★R★A★V★I★T★Y

> Gravity is a natural corporeal attraction between bodies toward a connection, so that the earth attracts a stone much more than a stone attracts the earth.
> —Johann Kepler:
> *Astronomica nova*, 1609

> Gravity and lightness are only attraction and flight. Nothing is naturally heavy or light.
> —Giordano Bruno:
> *Del infinito, universe e mondi*, 1584

PILOT

he was the sky
the endless space
he flew through
modulated
with plumped clouds
havens moisture-pots
dreams without
gravity

hurled out of consciousness
here
embraced by this plane
aluminumed bird
motored beak spinning
pulling him
sliding him
up and down the wind
through fatted clouds
through white
flopped onto white

he was all of it
and the ground below
that prevented
the clouds from
metamorphosing
the earth
even

up beyond the last clouds
where the air was scattered
by wind cleared of wet air
blued then black-blued
finally all black
where there was
no air at all

peace promised by
religions of priests
here hugging him
whispering about time
but there was no time
no angst
no gallons per hour
endless
keep going
fly on around the globe
again and again
or not

fly onto and off
this tangent
into that space
beyond clouds
and air
and time
and any of the others
and himself
beyond the others
and himself

finally
he was unnamed

born alone
without parents
perfect

IN THE FALL, FIRE IN THE TREES

The colors of fall roam slowly through the trees,
starting into the green of the leaves,
inching their way through this season,
catching on like love—until that time when
even love becomes nothing, as mysterious and

certain as the changing of the colors. Look:
this is the kind of fire that measures tones:
the yellows—see them high up along
the fringes—like four-year-olds mixing
fingerpaints, testing every hue and shade, free and

uninhibited. Now they begin to fool around
with those outrageous oranges; next,
the older reds and purples. They scamper
sprightly, kids almost out of control.
Ssh, quiet, listen to their chatter:

they prattle and tattle about the browns.
The sky's not quiet either; greys are
folded, jammed by an impatient wind
skidding through. It pulls patches of blue
in behind the rain; the heat from it all

makes me close my eyes until I reach
through your arms, pull you to me
and murmer how much this October means.
And in front of the fire we will be alone;
no one or nothing else will matter.

CUMULI

When I was small
I asked my mother what clouds were,
why they came and where they went.
She said she didn't know exactly
but I might learn about them one day.
Maybe they were huge puff balls like
the ones in the glass jar
on the table in her dressing area,
or even mountains made of pure cotton.

I would roll over and over on summer grasses,
next to the rock garden and games
where I built mud and
stone dams, rivers flowing from
the garden hose, great wars I staged,
bombs made of sticks
I unleased from my toy airplanes,
the unsuspecting bad guys getting it
every time.

And they would be there, billowed
and overflowing, splendid and satisfied,
big and silly, often with clown faces.
I would pretend I was lying on them,
or leaping from one to another,
doing the same kind of rolls
I would in school
when I ran as fast as I could across the mats,
jumped high, tucked in tight,

a ball of me without gravity, without breath,
as if I had the power to be anything,
a bird, a pilot soaking in the wind,
the freest of all things in the sky.

And in those wonderful moments
I could soar
above the rules of parents
or teachers or older cousins,
as if I was a little cloud
that could come or stay or go
whenever I would choose.

POND BAY, B.V.I.
FOR HERB AND MAR MEADOW

Here, giggling next to me,
pint-sized waves flop
on top of the tanned sand,
the newest infants
whelped out of a fleshy sea
that mumbles about the good old days
when no one sat and wrote
about ebbs and flows,
swings, sways and swags.

These baby rolls curtsy
like young ballerinas,
draw serendipitous lines
where they wish to be remembered,
swash marks with serpentine edges
in front of huge black boulders
flung here eons ago
and since washed smooth
by the water's incessant motion.

Red-veined sea grapes,
prickly-eared cacti,
all their local friends and enemies,
vie up and down the shore
for the best views.
Above the wave lines,
bustling ants
like messengers on missions,
ply routes only they carry maps of;

I pretend they form caravans
crossing great deserts
where the weak are slowly
baked without mercy.

In the sky of competing persian and indigo
mushed clouds gather in groups
and like the ants
glide on a specified course and
hitch rides on sliding air.
On the surface white-bounded sails
billow and strain,
stretch for the wind
pushing from the southeast
to pull sleekened sloops,
ketches, yawls and yachts
across the turquoise, and
around brown-green islands
planted strongly in the sea.

I have been across the horizon,
walked on land that burned until
it bled and screamed. Here,
so disparate, I can pretend
time is elsewhere, that I can remain
in this sanctuary for all my days.

TURN-ON

This morning darkness lingers...
Simple things are hard to describe:
the way the light edges over
night's borders, dawn one step behind,

the sharp, green-black silhouette of
evergreens pressed onto brightening sky
like the cut-outs
I used to make in third grade.

And there's clear, luminescent Venus
hanging from a string
below the sliver moon,
the only lights
still left on the blackness;
it's an odd configuration,
meaning something I don't understand
but meaning something.

Yellows and oranges wake up,
push into the darkness
like consciousness aroused;
and magenta flaunts its outrageous pink-blue,
even a band of green, if you look carefully....

Across the bay,
fire
climbs the windows of the houses,
dawn shakes loose, clears its sleepy throat.

And yet...
There are dim blurs on the water
not wakened by the wind
ruffling the surface,
perhaps flocks of scaup asleep or diving.
I can't be sure.

Before I can tell you
all that I have seen,
this spent night has journeyed on,
chased by morning
and my love that seeks
people, animals, everything—

and especially you.

REFLECTION

Rain is hardly itself,
but reflects
something else.
It makes sounds
only when it feels
what it touches.

I cannot see
rain
spilling
into my eyes.

The rain I know
stops at the bottom
of its trip,
as you did
when you finally
crashed
into where you fell,
turning like rain
into something
I cannot see
but only remember
as best I can.

Why couldn't you
linger
in the reflection

of what you said
at the end:
"Love, forever."

IN THIS HOUSE

The three of us,
The man, the woman, the child
Move like dancers
Toward one another,
Touching, hands entwined,
Balancing so that each can
Pirouette or jump or fly;
Then away individually to
Leap across our separate times
And seasons, always knowing
Where the other is.

When I enter our kitchen
She smiles, confirms
Old convictions that
She is the nest builder,
Prepares our food and
Cooks with the warmest hands.
She knows exactly where
Every item is, what must
Be done today and tomorrow.

He runs around, secure
This house will stand,
That we will envelope him
With warmth in ways he requires,
His world small and secure,
To be played in endlessly,
To be learned about,

His errors and fears accepted,
Discoveries boundless, wondrous,
His face lit up as it was after
Those first steps without holding.

I am the hunter, returned home
With provisions over my shoulder,
Come from finding the wind,
Feeling I have become
A weather vane,
Ideas caught and
Splashed from waves of the galaxy
So that each night I will dream
In a life I have borrowed
From a pure white hawk
Who cries in his dreams of me.

ORANGE CRATE ON A DAWN PATROL
vs.
THE RED BARON

FOR CALVIN

There was no question it was our
Spad fighter; we could sit in
the two openings (so what if real Spads
were built for only one), my brother
Calvin, eleven, and me, eight,
Errol Flynn and David Niven, taking
turns flying (the other was the gunner)
and wearing Dad's helmet and goggles,
ready once again for The Dawn Patrol.

> One behind the other, pilots, warriors,
> *good guys*, waiting for a chance to
> have it out with the Red Baron, Hun of Huns,
> Manfred von Richthofen (or Eric von
> Stroheim, it made no difference),
> sneering, intent on plucking us down
> from heaven, to be confronted in
> fierce aerial combat, the vanquished
> cut down like saplings before their time.

Their Ace of Aces terrorized the skies,
would seek to add yet another shtupid
Americaner to his eighty kills,
courageous but unweaned pups, flight training
limited to a pitiful eight hours,
thrown into the battle over Verdun or Argonne,
losses of pilots staggering, flowered
youth burning in their Sopwith Camels,
Spads, Nieuports and *them*, falling down
in their Fokkers, Hansas and Albatrosses.

Every night frantic calls from H.Q.
to our Flight Leader (Basil Rathbone,
no doubt) for yet another raid.

He would summon us from our nightly roistering
and order a strafing of observation
balloons, locomotives, troops or an attack
on a German aerodrome, *their* planes lined
up for sinister men, mustached, evil,
laughing, Allied blood dripping from
their Doberman/Police Dog mouths.
The skunks, vicious villains all, weren't
going to shoot us down. We would challenge
their best, the Red Baron, pry him out
of his lair where he lurked behind some
ephemeral German cloud waiting to pounce,
the sun at his back to blind us and
we (all of a sudden) on a mission of mercy,
flying serum to our brave soldiers,
wounded and languishing in a make-shift,
rat-infested field hospital, now
surrounded and being attacked by *them.*

Well Herr Sauerkraut was in for
a big surprise, all right, he would
have to face the Axinn Brothers,
dashing and exalted Knights of The Sky,
lionized aviators of the Escadrille
Lafayette (our mascots, the lion cubs
Whiskey and Soda, often riding with us),
skilled aces feared or revered along
the whole Front (depending on whose
side you were on that day), about whom
it was said acrobats marveled and copied.

Okay. It was to be The Dogfight of
Dogfights, about which an epic tale
would travel at least as far as the
dinner table that night, listened to
by our parents and five-year-old sister
(wasted on her, what did she know about
anything). There he was, von Richthofen,
in his bright red, three-winged Fokker
(some dude, he had to paint his *red*),
like a hawk screaming out of the sun,
a falcon with his talons extended,
bullets blazing, hot lead ripping into
our fuselage, the tapping, drumbeat
as the pattern came ever closer, until
one then the other was hit in the thigh
or arm or shoulder or anywhere but not
badly enough (even though the pain was
almost unbearable) to prevent us from
executing a clean sideslip (the maneuver
we knew from experience was the one
needed to dodge this cold-blooded beast
of the air who preyed on the righteous).

    Around and around, the fury of
    a maypole dance; twists, fake spins,
    Immelmann turns, incredible loops,
    dives, rolls—each angling to line up
    the other's tail in his gun sights,
    the sky a hot inferno for this play of
    death, bursts of bullets just missing
    engines and pilots, skill, and some luck.
    Finally his guns jam, he pounds at them
    furiously, his plan of another kill finished,
    the final nightmare upon him.

We have him, a varmint cornered.
I am about to administer the "coup
de grace" but my brother (he's a captain,
I'm only a lieutenant) taps me on
my shoulder as "The Baron" waits
for his ignominious end.
We fly alongside, our gallantry
and chivalry suffusing the two planes,
a certain glow perceptible from
the ground as thousands watch in awe.
We salute the "The Ace of Aces," he
motions for us to land with him in
the meadow below, and as we vault
from our cockpits, he runs to meet us
halfway (it's always exactly halfway).
He stands for a moment, not sneering
anymore, removes his leather helmet.
Silky, blond hair tumbles against
the finely chiseled features and erect
carriage of a Prussian aristocrat.
He smiles, salutes, his heels
clicking together in that wonderfully
precise way, then shakes our hands strongly.
"Ya, goot, der flyink, you are zehr goot,
vunderbar," his crisp, blue eyes probe,
search into our brown ones.

    Slowly he removes his gleaming Blue Max,
    hands it to us with great pomp and
    bows, while we, not to be outdone here
    or anywhere, look at each other, then
    bestow upon him our Croix de Guerres,
    Legion of Honors, Victoria Crosses, etc.
    Handshakes, exchanges, more salutes, waves.

We had not downed him but he was ours.
And the world would know that our fighter
of fighters, the orange crate, was superior.
Smirking, we carefully paint on its side
a small, red, three-winged Fokker.

MIAMI BEACH ART SHOW

This morning I whacked

the hell out of yellow tennis balls
high into fatted clouds, white,

fluffy and flopping all over
the sky as if playing was all they

intended to do with their lives.

Later, downtown on Collins Avenue,

a Sunday afternoon art show. I brushed
against the old, the stench of fear oozing,

blue-haired women, men whose jowls
have capitulated to gravity.

We are wrong. They are not stale
jokes or typographical errors

no one cares enough to correct. Nor am I
Michelangelo's Adam, touching the finger

of God on the ceiling of the Sistine Chapel,
a bit arrogant, convinced I can extract

pain and somehow undo lines
cut deep from cringing too much.

I cannot not smell their disin-

tegration, their eyes watering as
they shamble, unsteady, their gait waning.

They lead each other, step through
doors into rooms hung with pictures

where each life is painted on
a single canvas, one rectangle

that frames all that person was.
I hear them. So can you: "Boy,

that Morris, he was some businessman
when he was...once he was..."

And, "You know her, Sadie, she used
to be something when she was young."

And, "You heard? Hazel Fineman,
after her husband died...she sent

all her children, all to college...
now none, no one, helps her out."

It is painful to watch them
slowed by either dark or light as

they struggle to be included with the doers.
But they spiral down the well that sucks

time dry, and there is nothing
that I nor art can do

to retard their steady fall.

FORGETTING JESSE CARPENTER

We did forget your face,
        Jesse.
The one we gave you the
        Bronze Medal for.
When you did those things
        for us in
World War II.

Do you remember him,
        Jesse Carpenter?
No, of course you don't.
        Why should you?
He dropped out in '62, from
        his family.
From the way most of us live.

An alcoholic,
        Jesse.
The street was his home,
        with another vet,
Johnny Lamb, his old buddy in a
        wheelchair he wouldn't
Leave that last very cold night.

He froze about a block from the
        White House.
Where presidents decide how many
        hundreds of billions

Go for dams and defense.
He was easy to ignore
Out there in the dark.

THE SUCK OF THE GLADES

out there
beyond my child's eyes
I have stumbled into
a white night,
the inside of
a cotton-ball
prologue and
epilogue of
the nothingness
that will invade
my body and teach me I
will not be tolerated
on the inside of
this whiteness,
this place without
handles.

here in this
box of nightmares
I cannot see the stars,
touch leaves or
walk on roads
I know.

I am lost
over these
Everglades.

the engine is missing
and heating up.
maybe water in the fuel.
Switched over from
left to right tank,
pure gas may
calm her down,
damn, right side's the same.
plugs, electrical
leads to the mags?
okay, now she's smooth
and cooling down.
no, missing again,
what else?
nothing.

I remember making
wet tracks in
new April grass
but here
I leave not even
a memory.

I cannot raise
Key West or
Homestead Radio, if
corpses are manning
the air waves
I'll need to learn
to speak the language of
the dead.
this plane is fading,
falls slowly,

not strong enough
to save me from
the suck of the Glades.

I shout curses into
this white night
made from clouds
and if their bottoms
are not too low
I might find
a carved-out channel
to land in
or some lake near
the coast, away from
The Glades, their
rattlesnakes and
moccasins.

I can almost hear
the gators;
I will deal with
the mosquitoes.
just get me to the coast,
N99802,
so that they can find me,
come on, motor,
just a little longer.

what! yes,
out under the white.
coastline.
over there! where?
gone.... too far, anyway.
lower and lower,
oh, God.

have to land on
that brown-green marsh,
undermined by
coral that will tear
my pontoons, like
scalpels through flesh...
maybe not, if I'm lucky,
or if a prayer can
turn it into water.

voice of memory

I do not know
where you are, dad
I look for you
in the dreams
behind my eyes
or in throngs of clouds
whose language
I have not yet
learned
the silence
of thirty-three thousand
or three hundred billion
feet of ethered air
spread thick with souls
who flew away
before any had said
all they could
I miss you, dad
so many things
become memories of you
on hikes
holding my hand
in scary movies
safe on your lap
as you flew your plane
now I must take care
of myself
who
will take care of you

IN MY FATHER'S CLOSET

you do disappear
slowly out of mind
in your plane
        soaring
a hawk fading
        then gone
although I remember
standing on your shoulders
wrestling you let me win
going with you to work
those very last hugs
sometimes you understood
rodeos movies camping

your new things now ashened
there are fewer of them
shirts shoes jackets hats
your robes are waiting
        for you
or a visit from a son

I try
to remember
your keys will not rot
your voice and smells will
perhaps they already have

WHITE

Two short years ago
we met, then married;
now I stand long hours
outside your blanched room,
branched segment webbed
off the unyielding
purpose of this passageway
spotted with urine,
dripping intravenous fluids,
sap from humans
bleached and caught
in their square compartments,

        where time sits silently
        in the four corners
        like those harpies
        in Zorba, ominous, waiting,
        ready to pick away at
        whatever you are or were.

I pace, roam one far end
to the other,
probing, digging,
tearing apart where
I have been, where
I may be going
        with you or alone.

Find me the truth!
What is happening

on the eleventh
in the O.R.,

        where strangers practice
        the arts and sciences
        of plumbers, electricians,
        gambling the repair
        of defects
        in your faulted machine
        (see, the patient in 31B
        is wheeled to the twelfth;
        she is too white,
        her lease is up!).

The wait turns whiter,
vignettes unfold,
carefully planned
parts of a play
written for the ailing,
itinerant amateurs,
unconscious puppets
programmed for passivity
and drained of comic relief as
        they walk up and down
        their lives
        in this acrid quiet.

I meditate
midst their prayers and pleas,
squelch my hushed cries
for the way you were,
        close but as far away
        as another time,
        perhaps another life.

ANTIQUE STORY

Pilots are supposed to remember
to test and examine
their planes' parts before strapping in,
starting the motor and going up,
same as if cooking something
or getting dressed up to go out.
Think what happens when
you forget the salt, shave one side
of your face or leave your underwear off.

New, sophisticated airplanes
have checklists posted to instrument
panels but some of us who fly
old antique craft learned
to watch the float line or the cork
(no gauge or dial), feel the surface of
the linen fabric (now they're metal-
covered), stomp the ground to decide
if it's too soft (runways at larger
airports are macadam or concrete).

But then or now, you must drain
some fuel from the sumps to see if
water or dirt has settled at the bottom.
Your gas must be as clean and pure
as water promised in those Perrier ads,
bottled from a pristine mountain brook
gurgling down, its goodness and
sweetness you want and must have.

I forgot last week, the day I flung myself
the 20 miles across the Sound to Meriden,
a giant grasshopper jumping up
from Bayport. I was lucky, no problems.
Besides it was too cold to swim. And
life is a shaggy-dog story anyway.

DESERT, TUCSON TO PHOENIX

Mesquite mostly alone,
        looking like some argument
        no one listens to;
Saguaro cacti, ancient, like skeletons
        of medieval chessmen,
        branches and holes
        punctuated by gilded
        flickers and gila woodpeckers
        needle-protected nests;
Sagebrush in clumps, homesteaders
        pioneering on alien ground.
Mountains crouch on top of the desert
        floor, faces sharpened,
        their outlines sliced into
        thin silhouettes of
        mauves and steel greys.
Where water is spread, endless rows of
        cotton sing green on land
        baking in air so clear
        one hundred miles
        is close enough to touch.

I drive steering with my knees,
        an awe-struck kid,
        overtake a freight train
        two hundred cars long
        pulled by four locomotives,
        four identical brothers;
        it seems a little like
        my old train grown life-size.

Picacho Peak, Friendly Corners, Maricopa.
A small whirwind comes from nowhere, unexpected, scoops up
tan soil, spurs into a dust-devil.
Soon it fades away, as mysterious
now as when it was born. Somewhere there are jack rabbits,
rattlers and bull snakes, road
runners, bobcats, even mountain
lions but you'll not find them
unless you know how to wait.

Light crosses the range, fills places,
edging over, around, up, down.
It's like a trip through a lifetime. You sense more than you talk
and once in a while
you understand just a little
more than you did before.

STORM

The storm rises up
from its haunches like
a Doberman pinscher
seemingly trained by some plan
I cannot really understand,
seethes until its anger
no longer contained, springs into
a kind of morality play,
say, for example,
The Seven Deadly Sins,
which we cannot escape
as we are grabbed and
spun around by Thomas Aquinas
to stare into the snarling
faces of pride and envy and lust
and covetousness and sloth
and gluttony and finally anger;
and then this storm snaps its teeth,
slings foam-spewed epithets
across the bay, whips waves
to lash and claw at the sand
that stands braced for punishment,
then races up the banks
to rage through the trees that sway,
trembling, moaning
as if in contrition;
and in winter, it hurls hail
like bullets,
ice fingers that dig into your face,

force eyes down
as if you were guilty,
even though no one else concurs; then
you will prove the cold of loneliness
is judgment and retribution
but not necessarily absolution.

STORM SEQUENCE

Finally the roar
eases and releases you,
shaken, shivering,
humbled like an Adam or an Eve,
and the storm rages elsewhere
in search of other transgressors
who run and hide from its fury;
then serenity returns, the air
the sweet smell of a child
in your arms after its bath;
the quieted water is content
to lick the rocks and beach
as if the personality
of the Doberman pinscher
has been lobotomized out of
a golden retreiver's
who only wants to lick you
with the warming rays
of the sun fluffing up
a noisy bluejay confirming
the sureness of yet another
springtime you can inhale like
an underwater swimmer
who breaks through the surface
gasping breath and life again.

CLOUDS

are puffed-up
tales
telling stories,
illusions
whose time has come,

blown softly
by the Creator,
breaths
impregnating the air

the way
galaxies
are brushed
across
the cosmos.

THE FOG

oozes and creeps across the beach,
a giant hand of nothing, amorphous,
its fingers blurring dunes, moors and me.

What can I be sure of?
    Perhaps the direction
    I run:
        to the right
        the sun is oranged
        by time and hints
        of the dying day;
    under my steps
        the tide has yielded,
        the sand hardened and
        washed into tiny rivulets
        like thinned branches of trees;
    the surf lays down
        its carpet of water,
        edged in foam and bubbles
        that circle, probe and slide
        back to the maternal sea.

But I, I do not know where I am,
Enshrouded by this muddle of dim thickness,
Alone and so very lonely here in this fog.

THE WELL OF JACOB

I see the water
Down there deep in your well,
Jacob. The bucket drops,
The splash sloshes up the sides,
The same as when you heard it,
Jacob. Are you here,
Are you here with me now, Jacob?

Did you know who would come
After your water and after your
Jews, Jacob? Yes, the Arabs, then
The Greeks. And the Romans.
The crusaders drank here, too,
Jacob, filled with the passion of
The Cross they insisted everyone wear.

Your people, Jacob, they drink
Again from the well you once made.
I raise the bucket, it is heavy with
Blood and tastes of my soul, as it
Did yours, Jacob, here in this land
Men inhabit but rarely comprehend.

LATE MONDAY AFTERNOON, JUST BEFORE THE RAIN

We buried you
late Monday afternoon,
Dad,
just before the rain
but you
weren't really there.
We did it well,
like you lived your life,
now closed inside
the grained oak
coffin.

I looked for you
when I woke this morning
but you were shrouded
in the mist
of your mountains.
I could not hear
what you were
telling me,
the words were
slurred together.

Now, on this Monday,
a week,
you would say
I should not be afraid,
that I should

live with the pines
and the hardwoods
as they do
with each other,
I should watch
how the tide changes
and learn the ways
time passes.

I still see you
strong and confident,
high on your horse,
the one that does not
permit anyone else;
I remember
what made you
laugh,
when you became
angry;
I smell so many
of your smells,
hear your sure voice
in the dark,
miss your man's touch,
bristled kisses
and hugs we renewed
when I too became
a father,
when I too fell
fatally into time.

THE MEADOW

Early lift-off, I climb and seek
what's inside this bathed and bright morning.

Unloosened from the ground,
my wings are swan-like,

long and graceful, feathers spread,
I drink sunrise thoughts,

fantasies, and fly new day-dreams.
I'm high on spiced, fruity air;

eyes poke around the patches
on the blanket below,

land waves rolling on a fall sea, nature
resting after spring and summer work.

Hills rise up to view better,
streams wander to reach ponds,

families of evergreens gather
(they're all related by color),

back roads call upon quiet farms;
and off on the horizons,

the big fellows, the greyed
mountains hulk.

And then, there, nested in
folds of the land, a neatly dressed

meadow waits to be caressed.
I slip over to where she lies,

softly making my presence known.
Her shy smile welcomes, beckons and

I think I hear her say
"Dance with me."

We have never met but quickly whisper
we are already each other's.

I will leave the shifting sands of the sky
for what may be offered below,

whirl around and glide down.
She lays back as I touch,

gently, my wheels singing
across her body as I land.

GENESIS

You were not
supposed to be here
at the time
of my rebirth.
I did not expect
your eyes,
Hebrew-blue,
that I see
before anything else;
you must have come
straight from
the Psalms and Proverbs
after bathing in
the Pools of Solomon.

They will try
to stop us,
but we will race
across the forest floor
beyond their grips,
past timid ferns
swaying to lute songs,
past wildflowers waiting
thousands of years for us.
And at the end
of this pond
we shall throw
our pasts away,
slip down inside

each other's eyes.
I shall learn about my face
from your fingers.

You teach me
where warmth is,
deep inside,
where your shyness waits,
where gravity pulls me.
You make me shiver.
When my words tremble
you unravel them,
wiping away hesitation,
quieting my fears
muted by your faith.

I do not know why
you first said
"Dance with me."
Your eyes
are twin moons
that smile.
They have seen inside
and hint of the future.
We will go, then,
out there and
walk among the winds.

SUNSET ON THE AMTRAK, LORTON TO SANFORD

These pines are stiff and
          shiver with memories;
they smell the sweat of men,
they watch saws bite and cut
a swath
through the ancient stillness.
The pathway is double-lined
          in metal,
          gleaming and polished,
          clanged into place
          by hammers singing.

Join me on this journey.
You will learn to set the small
trembling fire of the hobo,
a blue-green lamp to eat and drink by.
Afterwards we will gather everything we are
to hurtle down the tracks,
rock back and forth like
you were by your mother when you were little,
          under the same pilgrim sky,
its pastelled colors
pulled west and down
          by the sun
          fatigued from
          pulling centuries
          across the eyes
          of all living things.

A silent wind crosses in front,
carries seeds towards the moist soil
of change.
Listen again to the whistle of the train,
to the cry of the pines.

OLD PILOTS IN SPRINGTIME

They assemble,
           these old men,
eyes searching the sky to know
what clouds would tell them.

The direction of the wind
is lined on their faces,
grooves like well-used runways.

A hand is rubbed across a face,
against the stubble of a beard.
They smell the fresh-cut grasses,
the moist and dew of renewal.

Soon they will lift off the earth,
again to touch the thickness
           of the wind,
again to hear the winged whistle
sweep across their ears,
their juices roused and flowing,
           these old men,
who would float on the wind,
who would curve through the clouds,
their aeolian sails brimming
for just a short while
until, like trees to be felled,
gravity brings them down,
branches to sag, leaves to die.

MALLARD'S WIFE

The mallard's wife waddles
To music I cannot hear,
Sneaks into the junipers,
Her nest cleverly hidden
In last year's fall leaves
But not the peeps and squeaks
Her babies make announcing
Their presence as if their calls
Were as significant as we think
Ours are.

A grey-haired couple follow
Their dog on the banks of this
Pond, old and green-edged,
Seurat-ed at the middle.
The mild breeze paints ruffled
Dabs on its flat surface,
The reflections of trees
Blurred like everything
In memory.

TREE
FOR NADINE HEYMAN

Do you remember when
I was little? You were my

comforter, a canopy with
wings spread wide, who listened when

I couldn't talk to *them*.
You were my refuge from spring rains,

summer's scorch and in winter
flakes of wet snow. I would stand

tight to your rough skin, your
thick body blocked me from the iced winds.

They couldn't hear
our whisperings and the things we shared.

If I cried you would touch me
or do something to make me forget.

When I climbed way up in your arms,
I was taller, more powerful

than anyone below.
I loved you in ways I could

never explain, and one day
you said my initials were yours.

I grew up, went across
the horizon, planted new trees.

Yesterday I watched them cut
you down, dump you on that

flat-bed hearse, your limbs gaping,
graceless, uncoordinated, awkward,

sliced into grotesque pieces.
I followed as they carted you

couched in your embarassment—
uncovered—onto Main Street

like a freak show for all to see.
But somehow, even after all that

you were still alive, juices oozed
out your sheared limbs and you lifted

a few leaves, waved into
a last wind. I turned from your

final humiliation,
unwilling to witness the very

end, after your last gasp, when
someone would warm themselves over

your burning bones, perhaps
laughing by the heat of your heart.

CHORUS

I want to tell you about the many
Who live inside me:
Several people of various ages,
Their clamoring like caustic cousins,
Replete with complaints,
Pedantries, Wagnerian vows.

The boy clutches old laments,
Embracing his past
Which too often is a stinking
But comfortable duty-diaper.
He distorts and
Romanticizes ad nauseam.

The juvenile hears only himself,
Accompanied by an ignorance
Growing as large as he does.
The young man roars,
An obstreperous lion looking up
From the bottom of a hill—

On top of which is the adult
Who must listen and attend them,
Hoping their bleatings become
The voices of men.
In the meantime, he will smile,
Clap and encourage them forward.

FORGETTING

The truth is
I forget them as they surely forgot me.
Their faces spread,
blurred into the white cream
of the cumulus I fly through.
Is it only four hours,
and one country ago?

I flee from their
Pavlovian smiles floating
over glasses sticky with lies,
Tartuffian tellings refined
into pâtéd clichés
that stink like ashtrays.

We may be our own allegories.
Our imprints and essences
melt like
the passion of leaves falling,
that flash before their grey crumbles,
before being washed by time into nothingness.

RETURN TO THE LONG TRAIL
FOR ROBERT MONROE PARKER

Wrapped in banter, we greet our trail,
Reach for the high ridge into air crisped
           with renewal,
Disconnected from everything we leave behind.
We peer down as we had that first time,
Thirty years before, youngsters flushed
But slowed by lungs and bodies grown older.
Yet Mount Abraham is still the same.

We lead or follow, brothers rebonded, trusting,
Joy swinging like our packs, heavy but light,
On shoulders and hips that remember and complain.
Time pushes the rain away, the valley unrolls,
Bathes green in clouds, silent prayers breathed
           into the mist.
Nothing is changed except what we have learned.

We sleep on boards of earth, voices hushed,
Night heavy with remembered whispers we need
           to hear again;
Far below a light sings of promise and mystery.
Morning is coffee and bread, eggs and bacon,
Hiking through wet, sweet and virginal mosses,
Evergreens shaped by the wind, rock ledges that
Offer views that make us feel we are
           among the gods.

Surely there is more, like streams gushing memories,
But we are content to come from the winter
Of our absence, to play old games in our
Mountains that lie back, arms spread, and shrug.

IN CLAM HEAVEN

It's been years.
I never thought it would occur,
something you wait for, half-
believing, a little afraid that
if you start to count on it,
you might jinx its happening.

Scuffling or treading with my feet
(clam rakes are not really sporting),
the first time this season,
anticipating *it* like those crazy trout
fishermen waiting for April first,
the thought of nailing that big one
who's fattened up all winter
in their minds like the fantasy
of a gorgeous young woman beckoning.

Pail in hand, feet at the ready,
toes concentrating on sand and mud
texture, sensitive to any firmness,
experience usually but not always
warning me about the difference
between a clam, shells or a crab
(a girl watches from shore, sees
a grown man doing the Water Island Shuffle,
interrupted every so often by little jumps),
or more important still, broken glass;
but cuts and limps from wounds
are marks of courage,
of sacrifices and dangers faced.

Yesterday
I was in Clam Heaven.
Didn't expect much; oh,
years ago before they assaulted
Great South Bay as if someone
had yelled something about a rich gold strike,
I used to have it fairly easy.
I used to have my special spots
which now I carefully avoid if anyone tries
to scrutinize a semi-pro clammer in action
(people do come over for the day,
youngsters hoping to sell a bag or two,
families convinced they'll have some
for dinner, everyone after *my* clams).

You know the rest:
it was fabulous, as if them clams competed
to get under my toes,
dozens, not small or marginal so that
I must calculate the minimum inch
of thickness; no, these were b-i-g
and fat, ready for the pot,
the crown jewels in a mixture of rice
and chicken, a few onions, and maybe
a touch of white wine or garlic—
Joan's Water Island Rice. Gotta go.
I know where you're going after you read this.
But watch it, buddy, you have to
be willing to die to get to Clam Heaven.

STALLS

A stall
is a ritual
of flying.

Pilots need to test
the exact moment
when gravity leans on
the plane's nose,
pushes it down
into a fall
and us with it.

To find
that moment when
change is in command,
the wheel or stick
is pulled back
as if we were choosing
to haul ourselves
backward into our pasts.

We point up and up and up
until the instant when
we cannot angle any higher.
Forward speed staggers,
time slushes,
we meet that very
second, and like
an orgasm exploding,

we tumble from
that held position,
wonderously out of control,
into the present tense
and, then, oh and then
into the future.

SEARCH

A short while ago, in another world,
I made a greened dream, impregnated it
with a peaceful ending.
                    Now, on the deck,
an insistent sparrow shouts in
a morning he promises will rival
those in Eden; beyond, the ocean
stretches its whitened edge up
onto the beach and the breeze
ruffles gently the moored dunes
while summer's concert of the sun
plays notes flashing on grasses.
Shine by shine, they shimmer in the heat
that lies down heavily on
everything in sight. And the blades of
grass move like dancers dressed
in tan for a soundless ballet.

I will survey the greens of my mind,
the seasons of my lives.
                    The past and present
are like pictures blinked, homemade
movies that unwind as I sit, vignettes
that swim through my nervous system.

Soon
      people cluster and spread
their lives out like unfolded blankets
they need to rationalize what they really do.

For most, time is filtered in rainbowed
light where words weave and tumble
like children performing with endless
energy. There are photographs, of course, as if
what's happened could be held in suspension,
and billions of messages are sent up and back
by them, to them, from them, for them,
around eyes and ears watching, deciding.
And picnics, too, perfumed pleasures
cherished and memorized for later.

                        Strange business,
existence, spread beyond and in front of
comprehension, planted for knowledge
gathered like grown wheat and sifted
in our minds over millions of eons,
mysteries with answers we have not yet
learned, our understanding metered and
registered—but never sufficient
to know what is on the other side of
                             eternity.

DAUGHTER'S FAREWELL

The brackish winds of March seethe,
beating the ashen water into
whitecaps and humps of froth.
What whip lashes the air?
Something unseen yet screaming.

My daughter stands at the edge,
distant and alone, blonde head
bared and bowed, shoulders rounded.
Her lover is being sucked into
the ground she tried to keep closed.

She would throw herself in,
scarcely hearing the prayers of farewell
washed white by iced rain, plunging
down on her lover being lowered
into his final bed of dust.

I miss mine so: lover, father, friends,
their faces masked, colored the gray
of yesterday, voices harder to remember,
hugs and smiles that are ancient memories,
bodies no longer able to pretend.

The wind tears pieces from my mind.
I sway, witness to the ceremony
she requires, this daughter of mine,
who practices much too early,
who must one day help me down inside.

TIME TO FLY

Soon they come, the pilots,
needing to get off the ground,
gravity oppressive, no longer
acceptable. They gather early
on this flat field, edged with
trees they know mark the limits
of the time they will have
to stop within or rise above.

Light has overpowered darkness,
lifting it off and away for the day.
Two, maybe three or four congregate,
a circle of comrades,
to poke the earth with small talk,
to share glances of the sky,
to feel the wind replace thoughts
until one says slowly,
as if he had drawn the winning card,
"Looks pretty good, I guess."

Then maybe a scratch behind an ear,
a grin, a nod, a turn toward
the hangar where a bi-plane
waits and listens.
The pilot rolls open the large doors,
walks to his flying ship,
its smells filling his soul
like an elixir. He stands for a moment
between the wings and fuselage,

rests a hand on the painted fabric,
its feel no longer needing
to be remembered.

IMPOSSIBLE TASKS
FOR MERI, ALLIE, MIKE, JENNY

I cannot teach you
        about death.
I cannot pass on to you
        what I do not know.
I can only imagine what
        the beyond is,
    where we have never been,
    where we presume something is,
        like light or time.

I do not know if anything exists
        past the last galaxy,
    in that void hardly contemplated.
How many is the infinite number
        of oxygen and hydrogen atoms
        that join to create water
            in perfect symbiosis?
What happens when endless zeros created by
        some giant computer
    go berserk and finally take over?
What happens when ticker tape is programmed
        forever and can never be stopped?
            And in greened Iowa,
The kernels of yellow-gold corn, are there as many
    as the uncounted stars in the uncounted
        galaxies?

Oh, but I will tell you
        that if death were
    an enemy, I would fight like hell.

We would engage in epic combat,
        roiling on
    boiling seas, clanging underneath
    Wagnerian evergreens, hurling thunderbolts
        across mountains
    My blows would be Herculean,
        my rage unstoppable,
My victory complete, death killed and
    cast under your feet.

But, it may even be that death is simply
        the nothingness beyond,
    beyond numbers, beyond thought,
        beyond fantasy,
Where time transcends anything
        we can comprehend.

    Or, death may live in a place
Together with life, where colors are soft
        and warmed with hope,
    smells the sweetness of pleasure,
Touch the security of faith, of peace,
        taste the sharp cockiness
    of confidence, and
Sight the laughter and tears, the love
        I have had
    since you came from that other place,
To be carried with me here and where
        I will go.

ABOUT THE AUTHOR

Donald Everett Axinn, the author of two previous books of poetry, *The Hawk's Dream* and *Sliding down the Wind*, has written poems and articles that have appeared in *The New York Times, Newsday*, and many poetry magazines, including *New England Review, The Poetry Miscellany, The New York Quarterly*, and *Writers Forum*, among others. In 1979 he was awarded the Tennessee Williams Fellowship in Poetry at the Bread Loaf Writers' Conference of which he is director of planning. He has been a university dean and arts institute director. In addition to being a writer, he is a highly recognized developer who has received many awards for architectural design and community enhancement. He is a director of Poets & Writers, special consultant for the *New England Review/Bread Loaf Quarterly*, trustee of Hofstra University, North Shore-Cornell University Hospital, a member of P.E.N., Poetry Society of America, and Poets House. He lives on Long Island, where he flies his classic airplane.

OTHER POETRY TITLES PUBLISHED BY GROVE PRESS

ALLEN, DONALD, and BUTTERICK, GEORGE F. (eds.) / The Postmoderns: The New American Poetry Revised / $9.95
ALLEN, DONALD and TALLMAN, WARREN, (eds.) / The Poetics of the New American Poetry / $12.50
ALVAREZ, JULIA / Homecoming / $7.95
AXINN, DONALD / Against Gravity / $5.95
BAUDELAIRE, CHARLES / Selected Poems / $4.95
BECKETT, SAMUEL / Collected Poems in English and French / $3.95
BECKETT, SAMUEL / Poems in English / $2.95
CUMMINGS, E.E. / 100 Selected Poems / $4.50
H.D. / Selected Poems of H.D. / $8.95
JACKSON, RICHARD / Part of the Story / $5.95
KEROUAC, JACK / Mexico City Blues / $9.95
LORCA, FEDERICO GARCIA / Poet in New York / $6.95
LUNCH, LYDIA, and EXENE CERVENKA / Adulterers Anonymous / $6.95
MARIANI, PAUL / Crossing Cocytus / $5.95
MARIANI, PAUL / Prime Mover / $7.95
NERUDA, PABLO / Five Decades: Poems 1925-1970, Bilingual ed. / $12.50
NERUDA, PABLO / A New Decade Poems 1958-1967, Bilingual ed. / $5.95
NERUDA, PABLO / New Poems (1968-1970), Bilingual ed. / $8.95
NERUDA, PABLO / Selected Poems, Bilingual ed. / $5.95
O'HARA, FRANK / Meditations in an Emergency / $12.50
PATERSON, ALISTAIR, ed. / 15 Contemporary New Zealand Poets / $9.95
PAZ, OCTAVIO, ed. / Mexican Poetry / $7.95
PINTER, HAROLD / Poems & Prose 1949-1977 / $5.95
STRYK, LUCIEN, ed. / The Crane's Bill: Zen Poems of China and Japan / $4.95
WALEY, ARTHUR (trans.) / The Book of Songs / $9.95

At your bookstore, or order below:
Grove Press, Inc., 196 West Houston St., New York, N.Y. 10014
Please mail me the books checked above. Offer not valid outside U.S.
I am enclosing $ _____ (cash or charge)
(No COD. Add $1.00 for one and .50 for each additional book for postage and handling.) We accept ☐VISA ☐MC ☐AMEX (choose one).

Signature _____ Number _____
Name_____
Address_____
City_____State_____Zip_____